INSPIRED

Compassion

Steve Parish & Kate Prentice

PASCAL PRESS

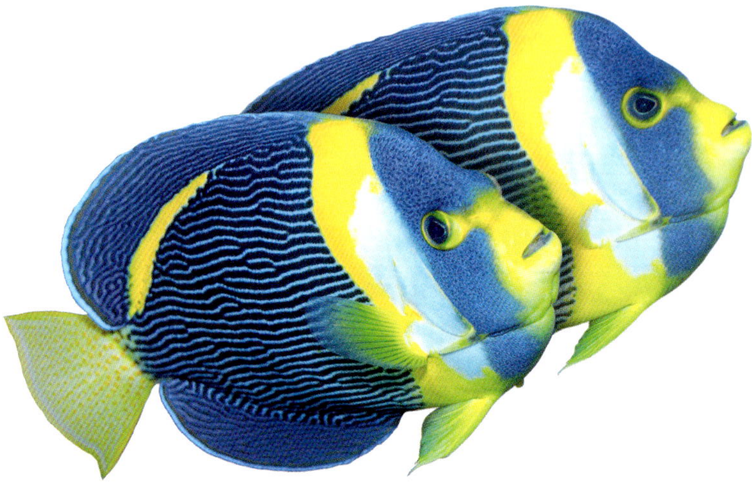

Compassion

Keeping us humble,

connected and caring ...

Introduction

In the process of awakening, of living in this moment, we feel connected to all things, and compassion flows for the suffering of others. Feel that compassion for yourself as well and treat yourself and others with kindness and mindful action.

This attitude will lead to an opening of your heart so you can live your life from a place of heart-connectedness. This will surely bring about a sustainable future for all.

Practise compassion every day using the mindful moments as a guide.

Steve and Kate

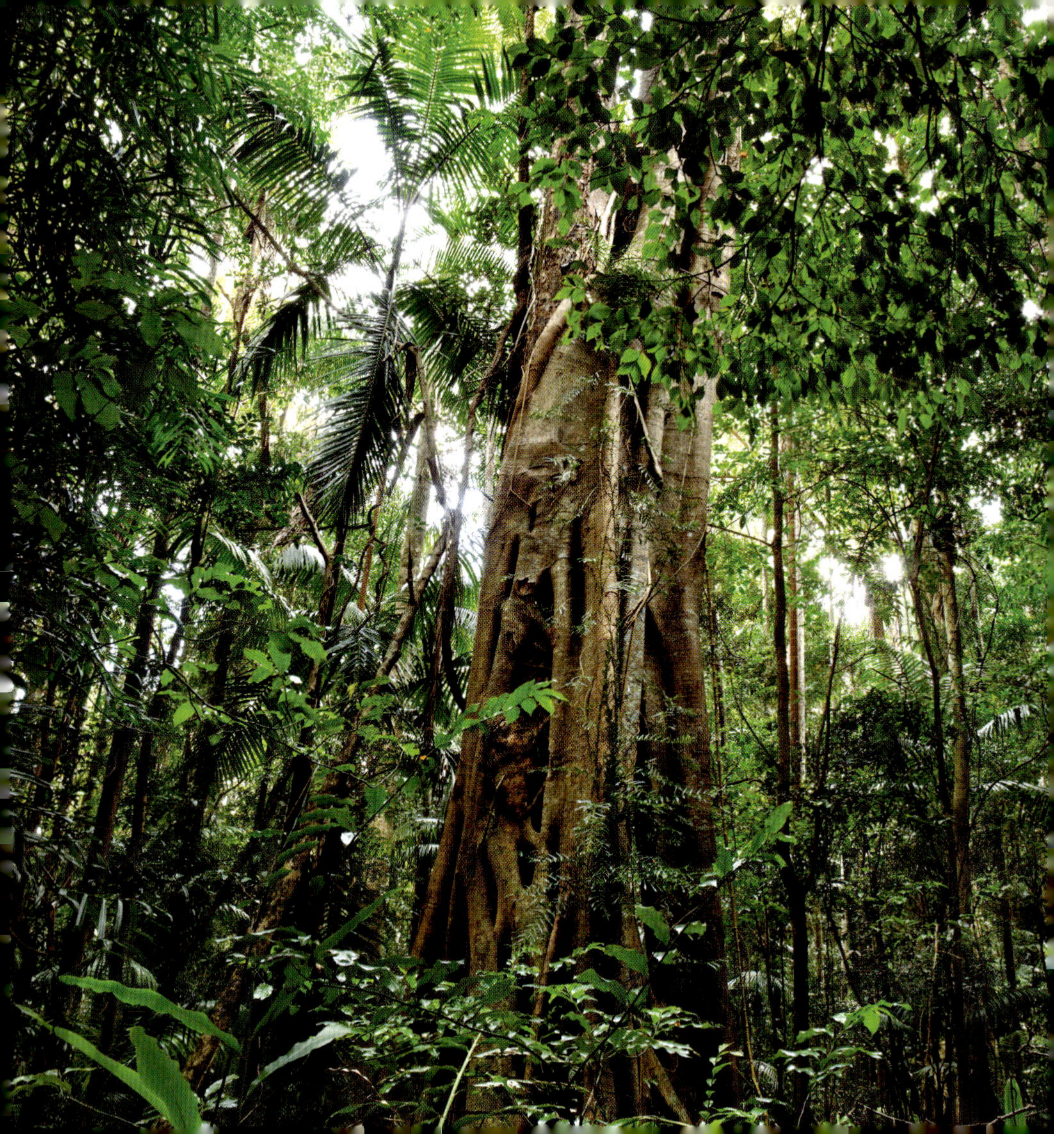

Contents

Compassion

Being

Connection

Generosity

Relating

Empathy

Humility

Forgiveness

Consideration

Embracing

Peace

Trust

Open-hearted

Awakened

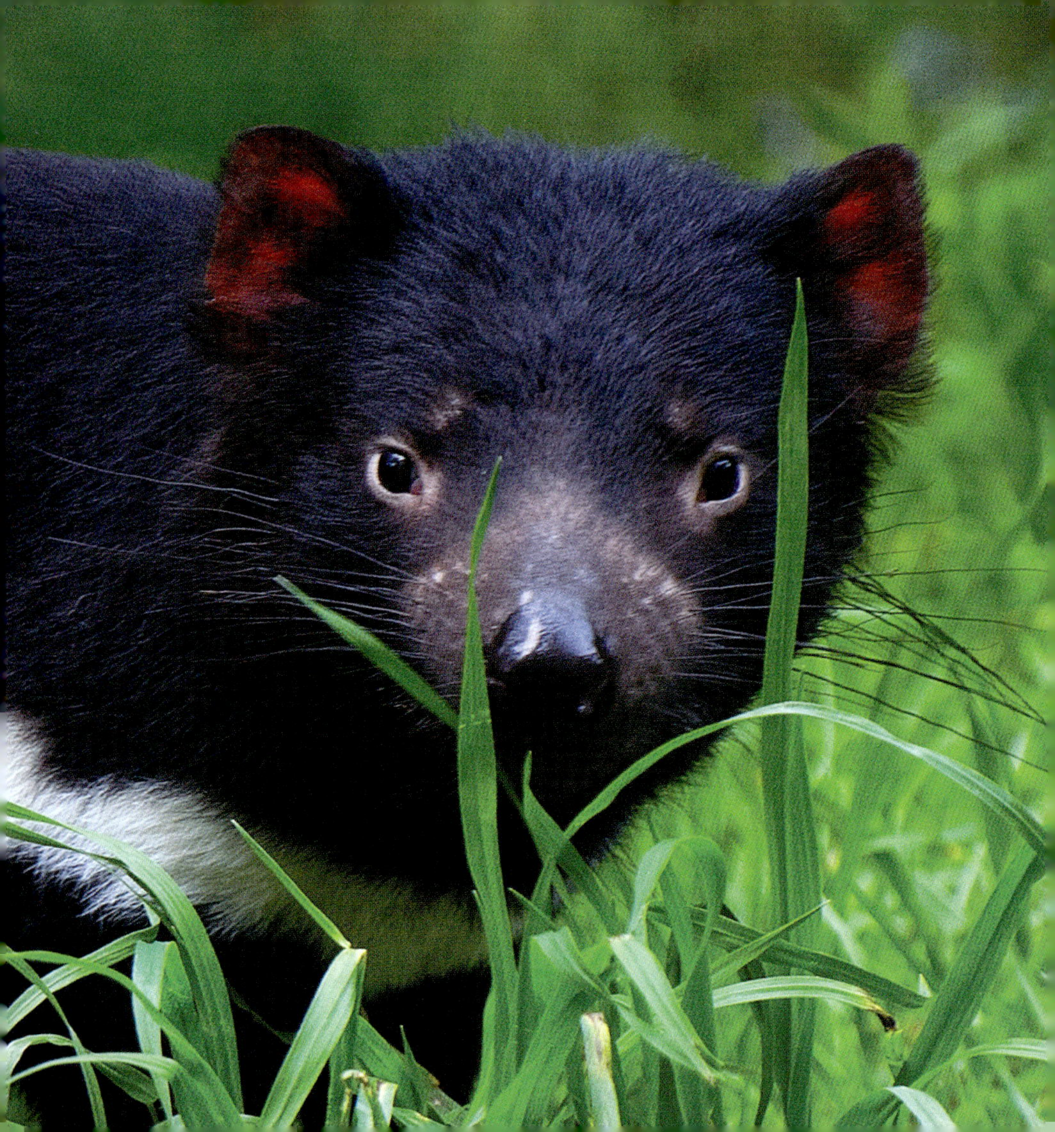

Compassion

*Until he extends the circle of his compassion to all
living things, man will not himself find peace.*

ALBERT SCHWEITZER

Compassion is having the insight to see and feel ourselves in others. When we realise our kinship with all life, we can move respectfully towards those that are suffering and take kindly action on their behalf.

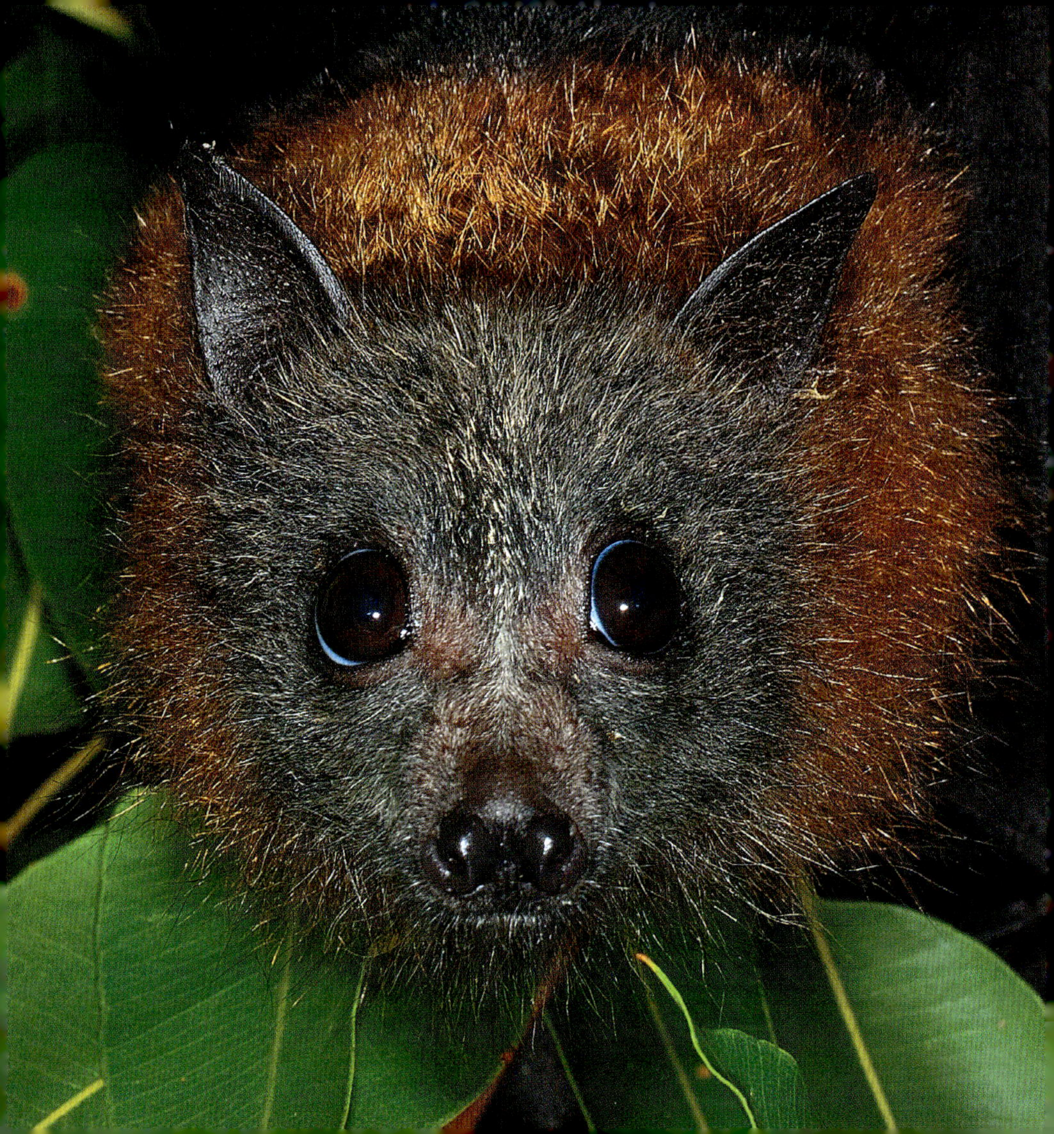

Take a moment for

Compassion

*Volunteer some of your time
 to help others in need*

Take action for sustaining animal habitats

*Have a compassionate moment
 for yourself everyday*

Being

*To be yourself in a world that is constantly
trying to make you something else
is the greatest accomplishment.*

RALPH WALDO EMERSON

Compassion is easier when we are in the present moment of 'being'. Be mindful that our thoughts can create separation between 'I' and 'you'. There is no separation in the eyes of the soul. The greatest gift one can offer a person who is suffering is compassionate action.

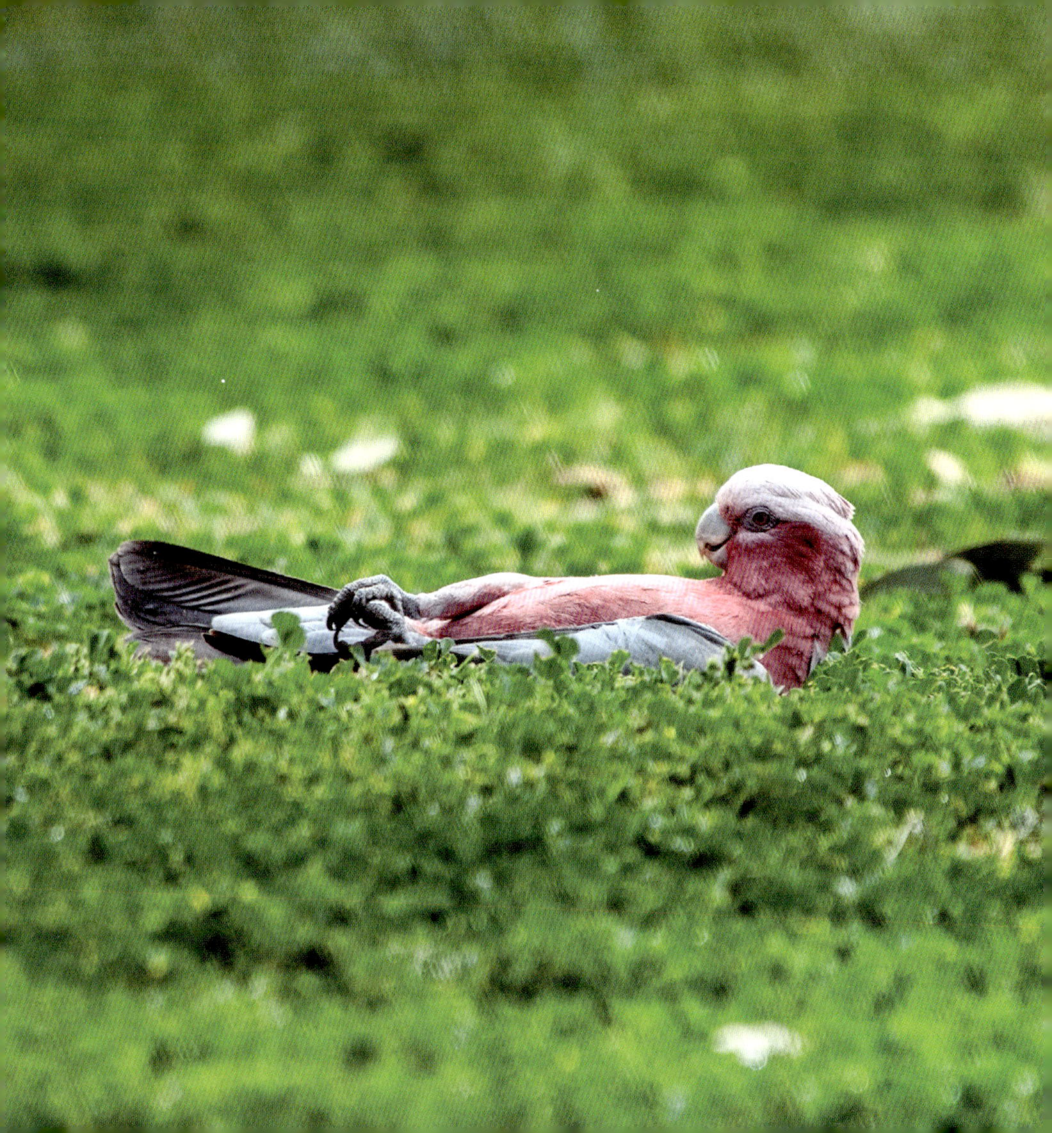

Take a moment for
Being

***Breathe** slowly and deeply*
while focusing on each breath

*Take a quiet **moment***
to BE in a beautiful place

*Bring 'being' into your **'doing'***
a little bit at a time

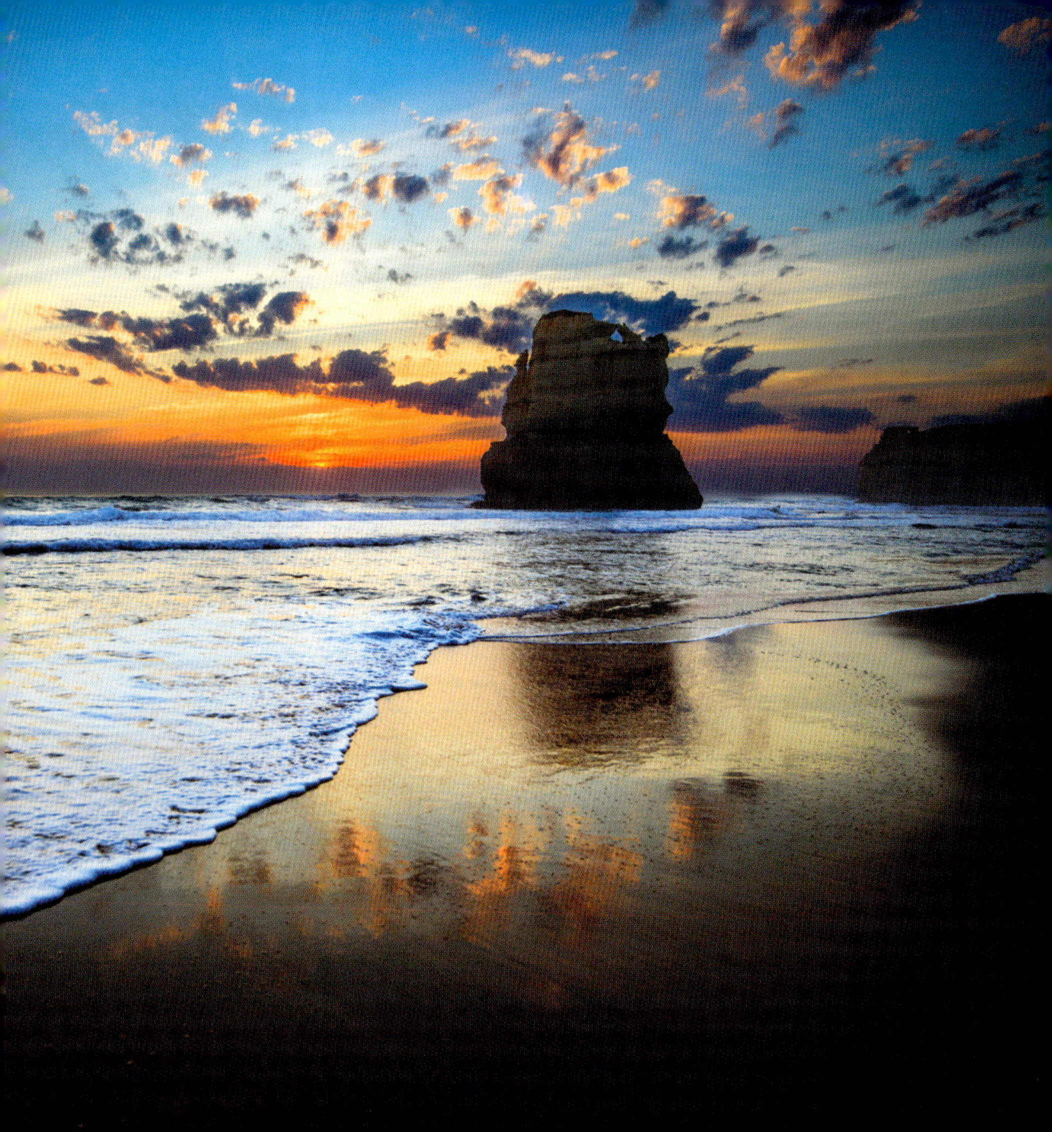

Connection

*You may say I'm a dreamer,
but I'm not the only one.
I hope someday you'll join us.
And the world will live as one.*

JOHN LENNON

All living things share a connection — animals, plants and people alike. At times we separate ourselves from others and nature, creating a community where the individual is seemingly more important. Remembering our connection keeps us aware of others and their needs, encouraging an attitude of compassion and generosity.

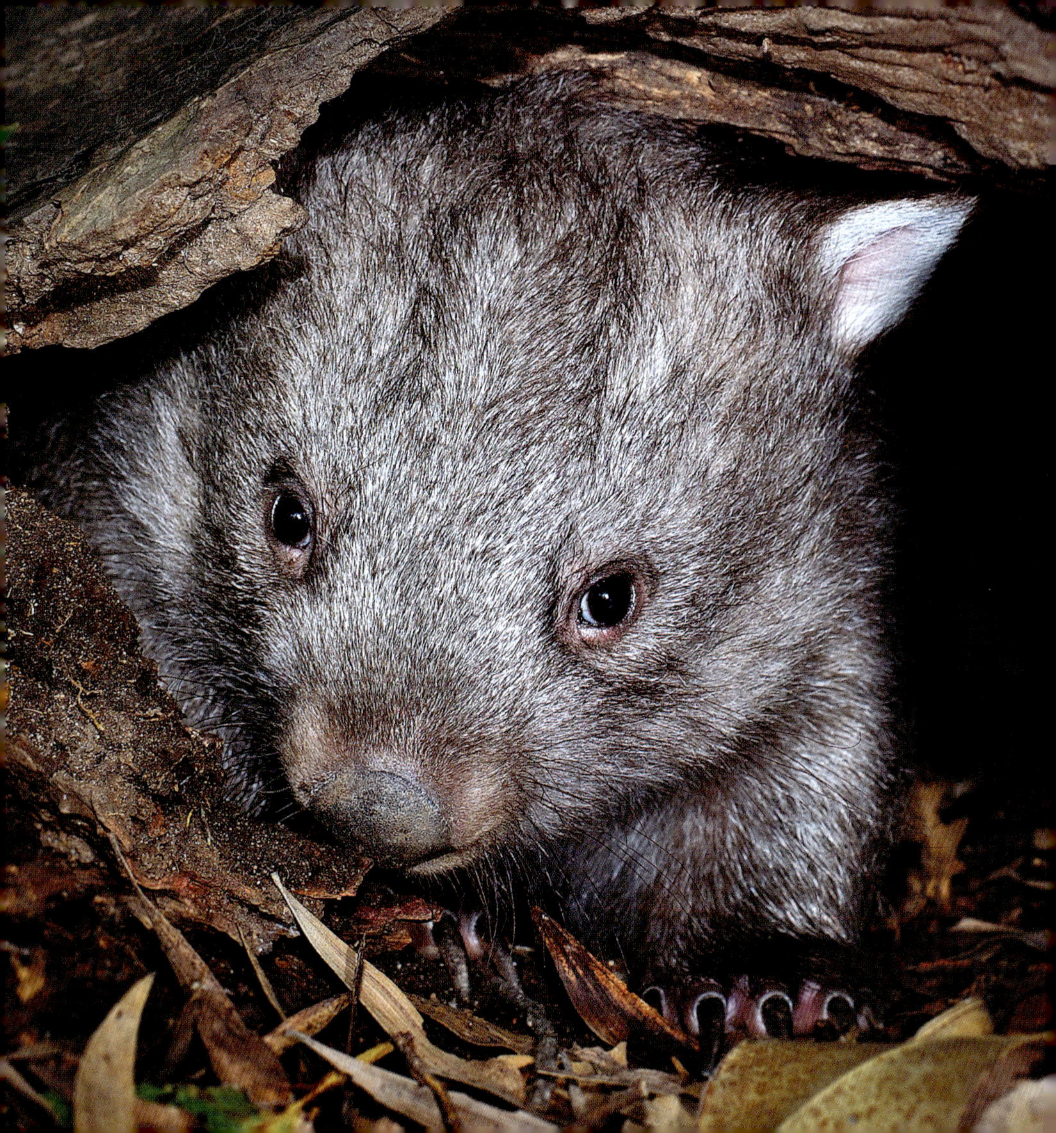

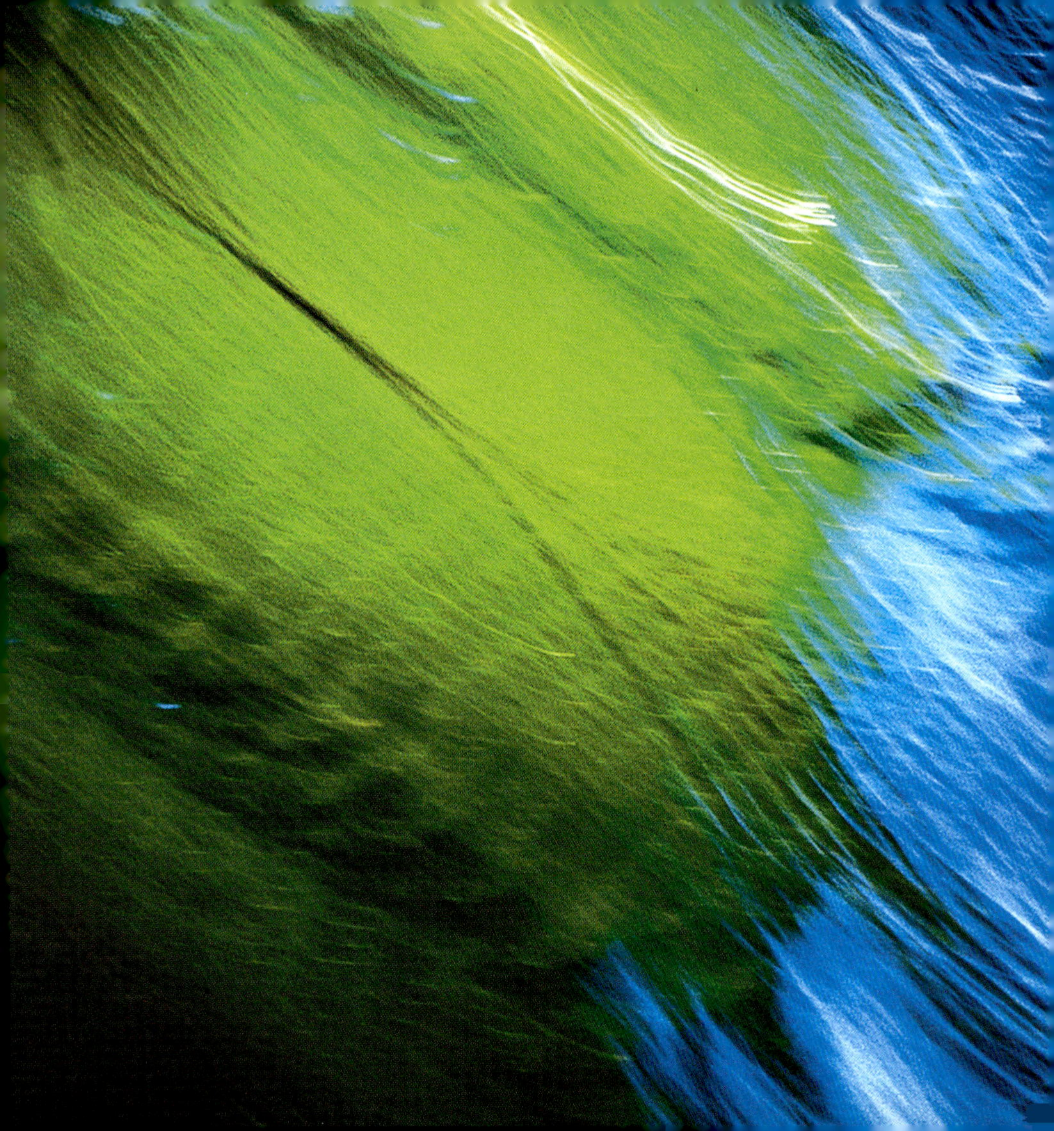

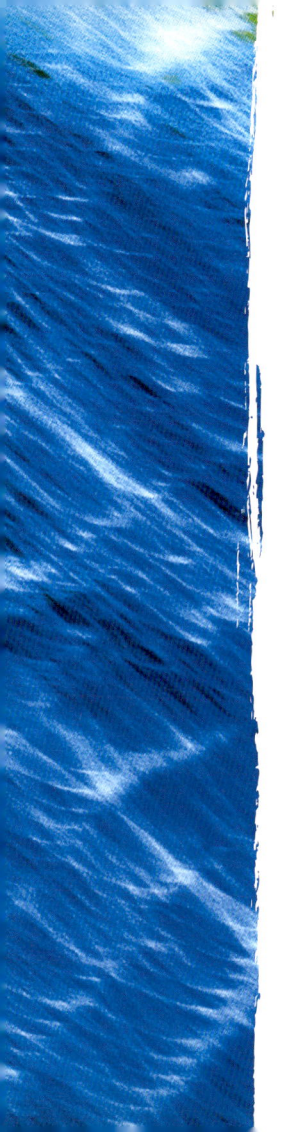

Take a moment for

Connection

*Walk barefoot in a garden
and feel the* **earth**

*Feel the connection between you
and a tree — the tree breathes out,
you* **breathe** *in*

*Look into the eyes of people you
speak to and connect to their* **souls**

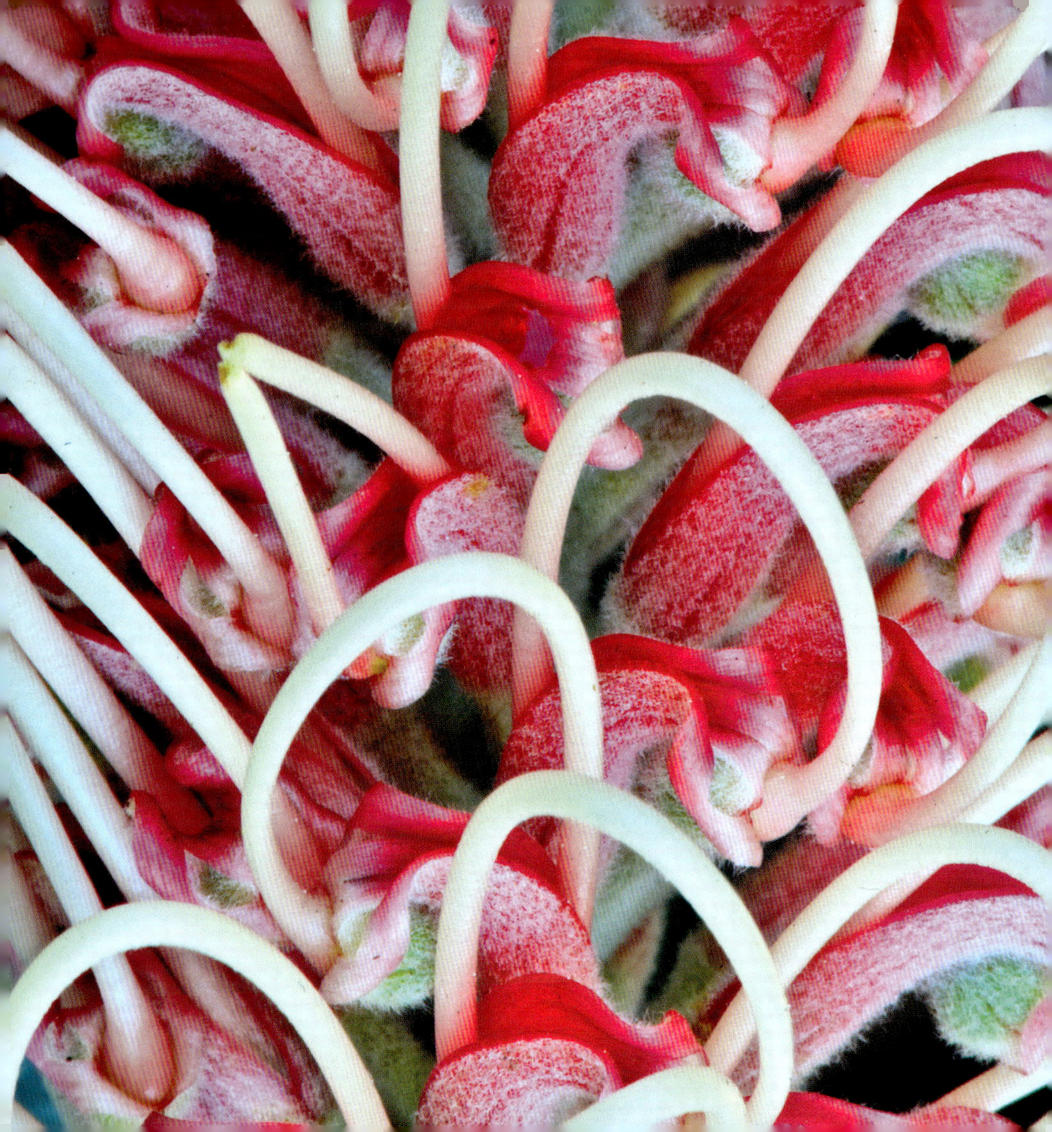

Generosity

No act of kindness,
no matter how small, is ever wasted.

AESOP

Give with your heart full of good intention — willingly and selflessly. Whether you give food, money, possessions, or give of yourself, your heart will grow stronger and feel lighter. Give all you can and, in turn, your life will be rich and full.

Take a moment for

Generosity

*Make a plan to donate your time
and **share** yourself with others*

*Be generous to your body
and **spirit** — you are precious*

*Ask **yourself**, "Who am I?"
and answer generously*

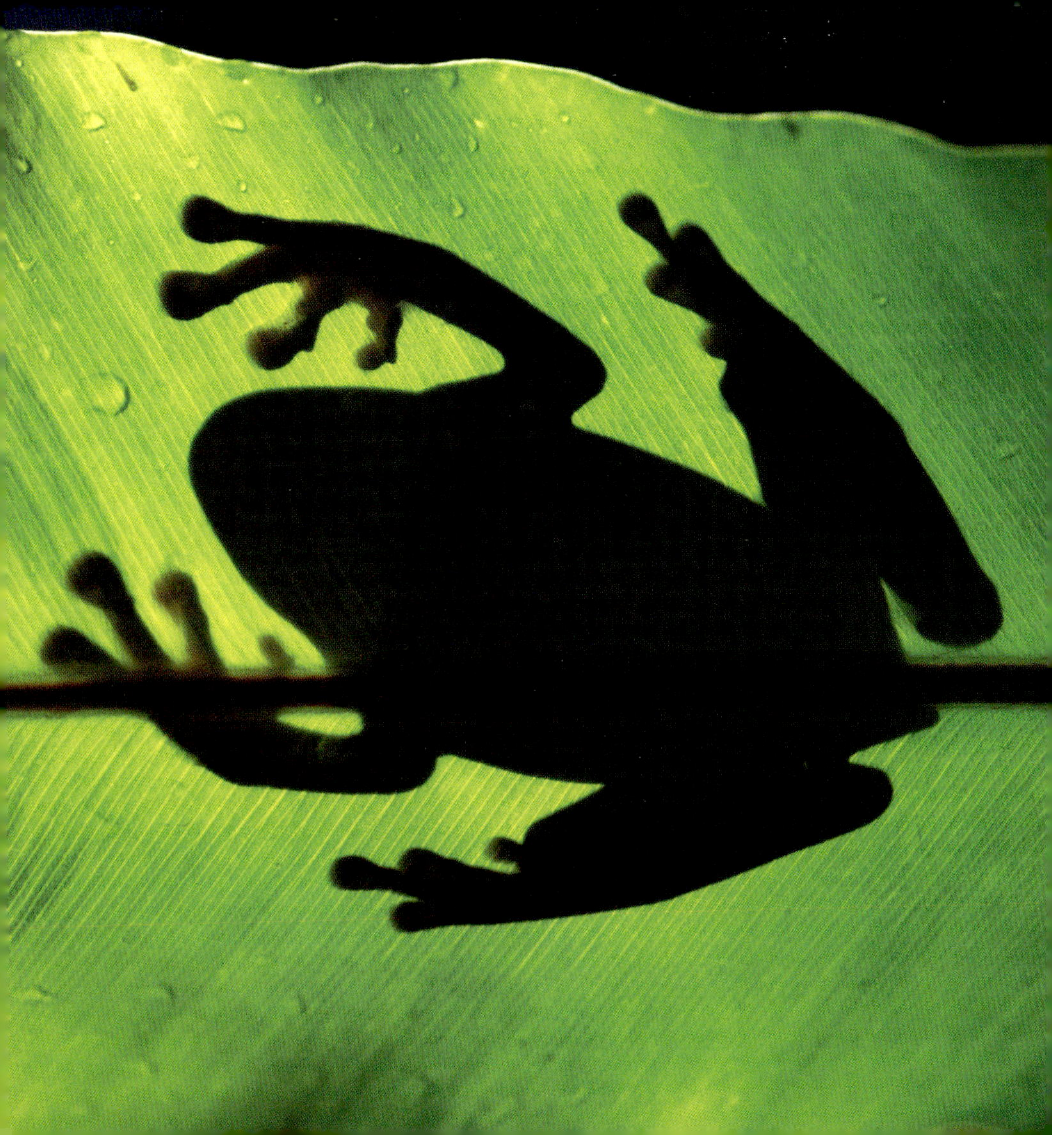

Relating

It is easy enough to be friendly to one's friends.
But to befriend the one who regards himself as your
enemy is the quintessence of true religion.
The other is mere business.

MAHATMA GHANDI

Relating positively to people and the natural world is beneficial to all. It is a connection that releases endorphins and feelings of well-being into the body and the mind. This connection is most beneficial when the heart rather than the mind is involved.

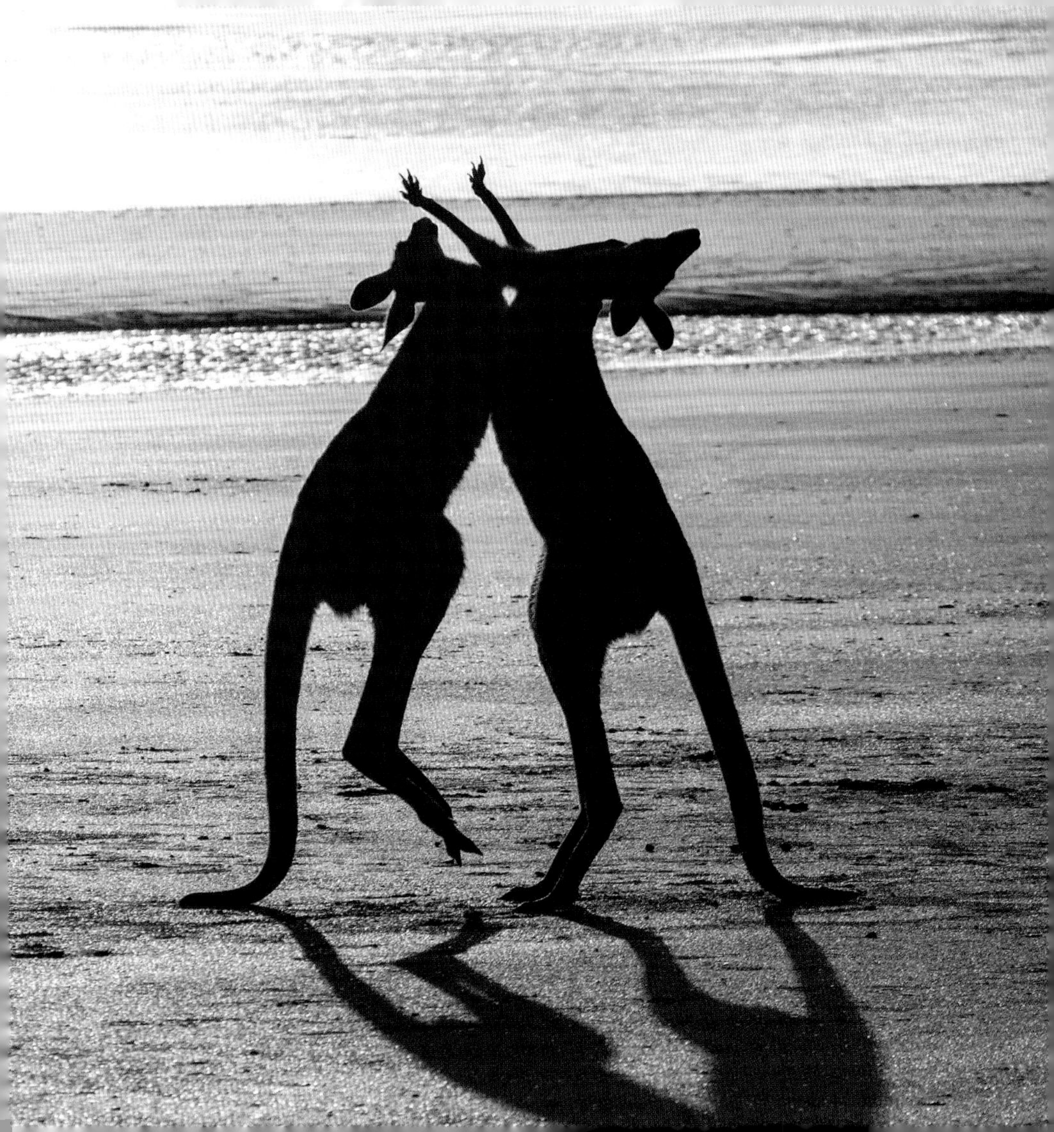

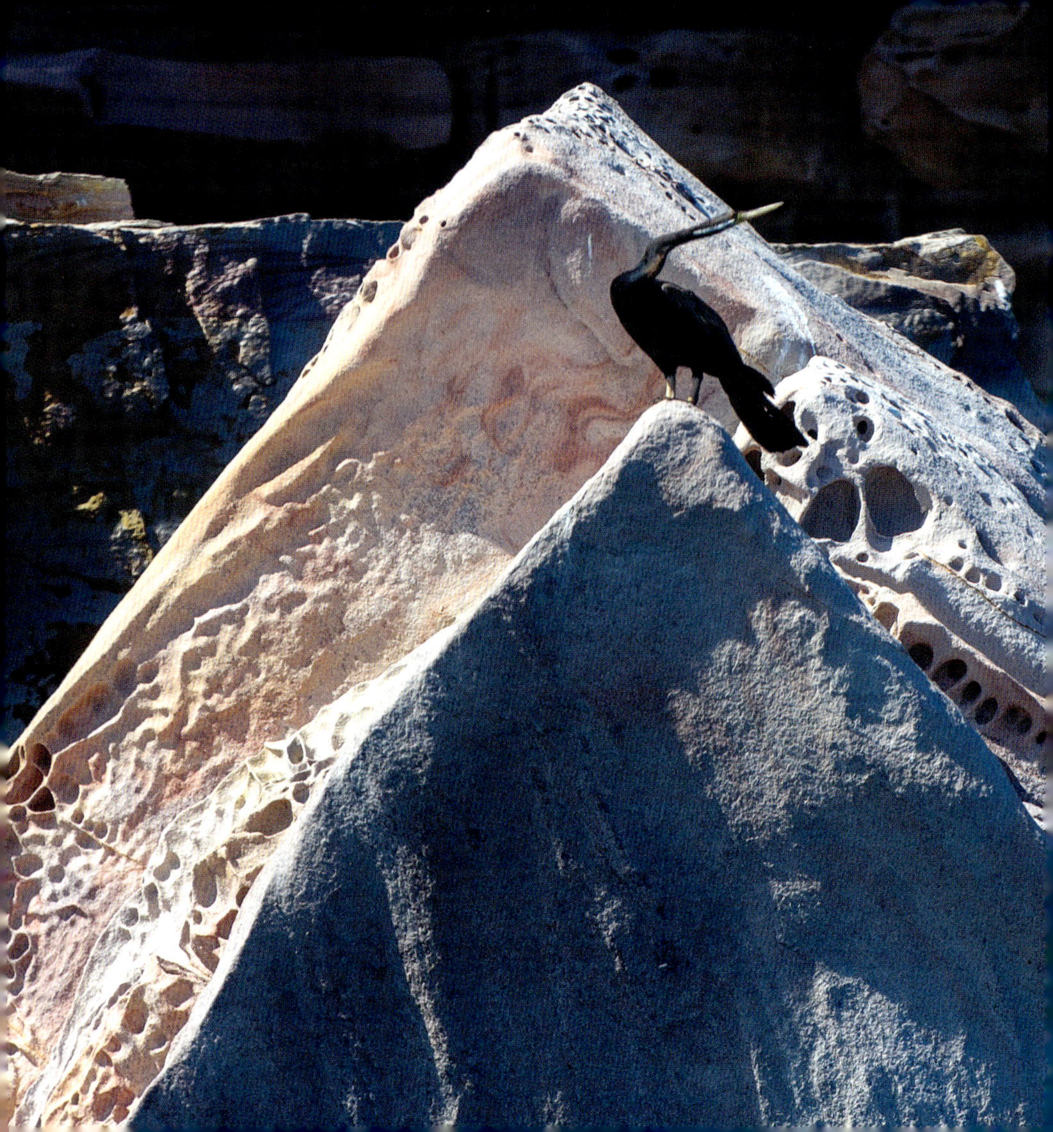

Take a moment to *Relating*

*Be **kind** to yourself in
your mental chatter*

*Balance giving with **receiving**
— like breathing*

*Sit quietly with an animal
and exude **peace***

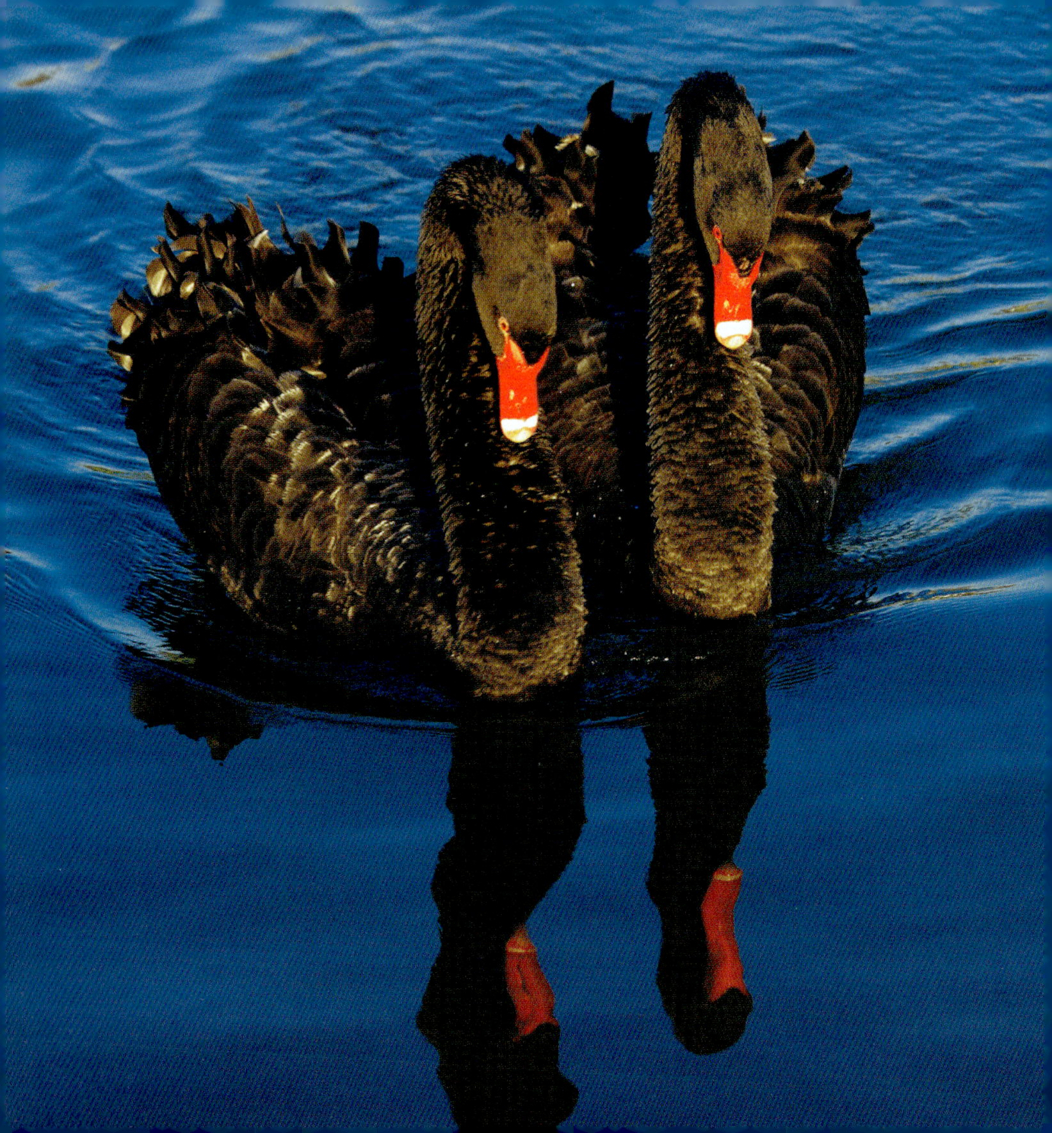

Empathy

The great gift of human beings is that we have the power of empathy, we can all sense a mysterious connection to each other.

MERYL STREEP

Expressing empathy towards others means understanding and sharing their thoughts, feelings and concerns. It is a selfless act which enables us to learn more about people and the natural world, and enhance our relationships with them. It comes from a state of compassion and open-hearted recognition of another's suffering.

Take a moment for

Empathy

*Become aware that when
 you smile inwardly, the person
  next to you will **feel** it*

*Take **care** of yourself when helping
 to alleviate another's suffering*

*Empathise with **creatures**
 that have lost their habitat*

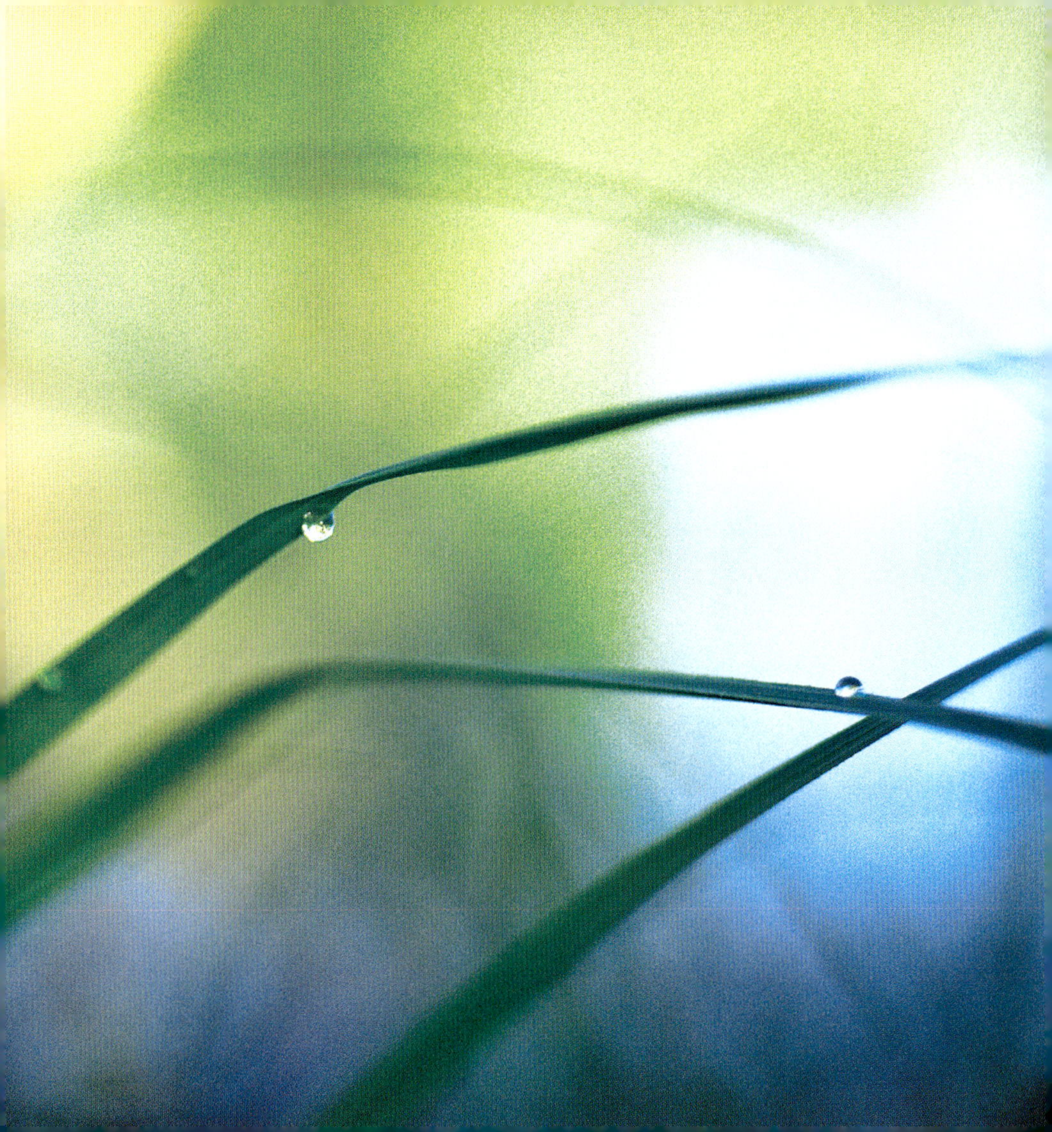

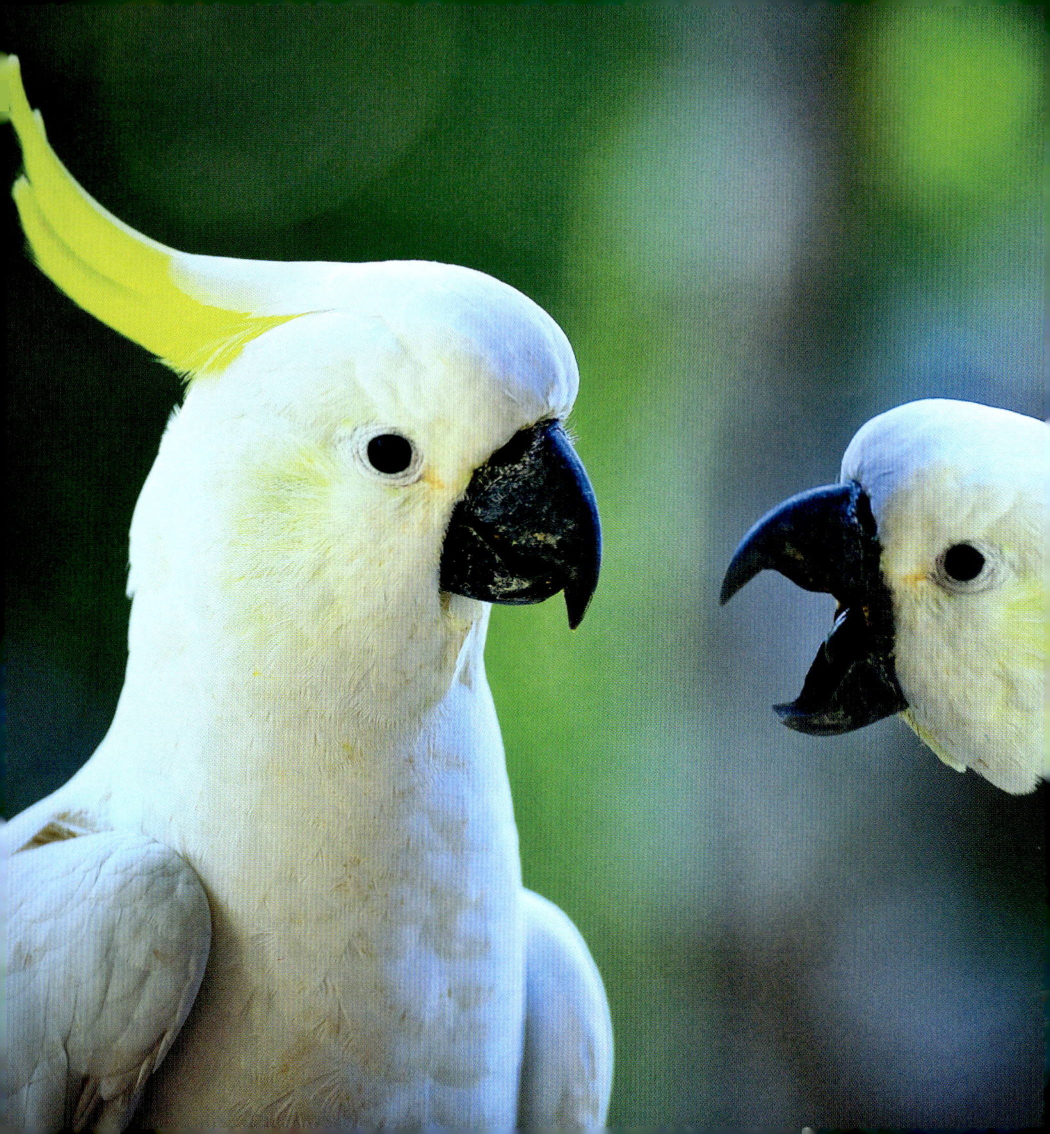

Humility

*True humility is not thinking less of yourself;
it is thinking of yourself less.*

CS LEWIS

Humility is gained from practising compassion. When our sense of self-importance is balanced, we recognise our own place, responsibility and contribution to the whole — then humility has been attained.

Take a moment for
Humility

Look to the micro-world as a reminder of our place in the **universe**

Be mindful of your place in the **natural** *world*

Do a simple chore for someone else with attention,
care and **awareness**

Forgiveness

*… In the space of letting go, she let it all be.
A small smile came over her face.
A light breeze blew through her.
And the sun and the moon shone forevermore …*

ERNEST HOLMES

Forgiveness is freedom and freedom allows compassion. Hold the perception that everyone is doing the best they can in life with the resources they have. By letting go of old issues from the past and forgiving ourselves and others, we are able to move forward in our relationships.

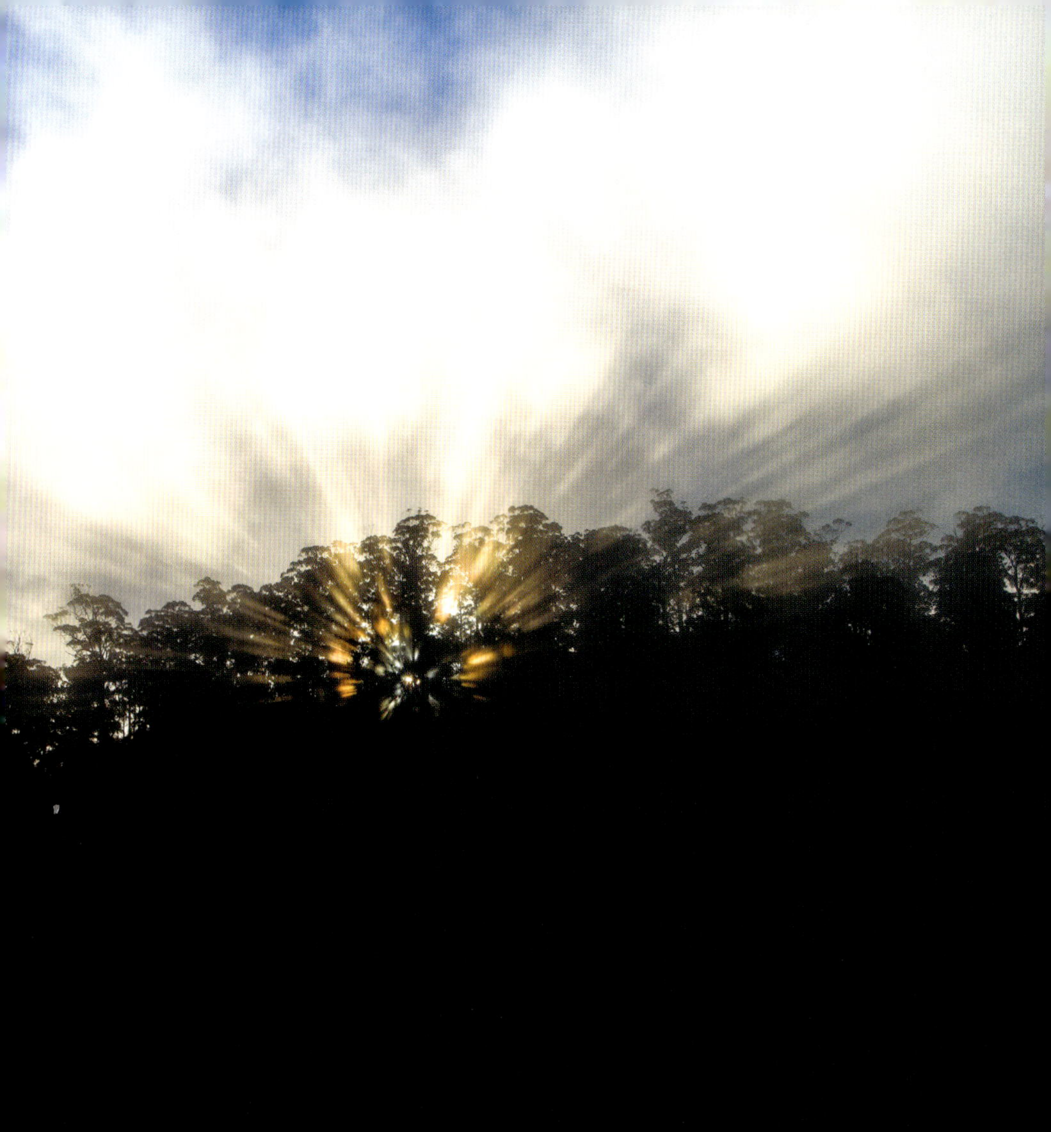

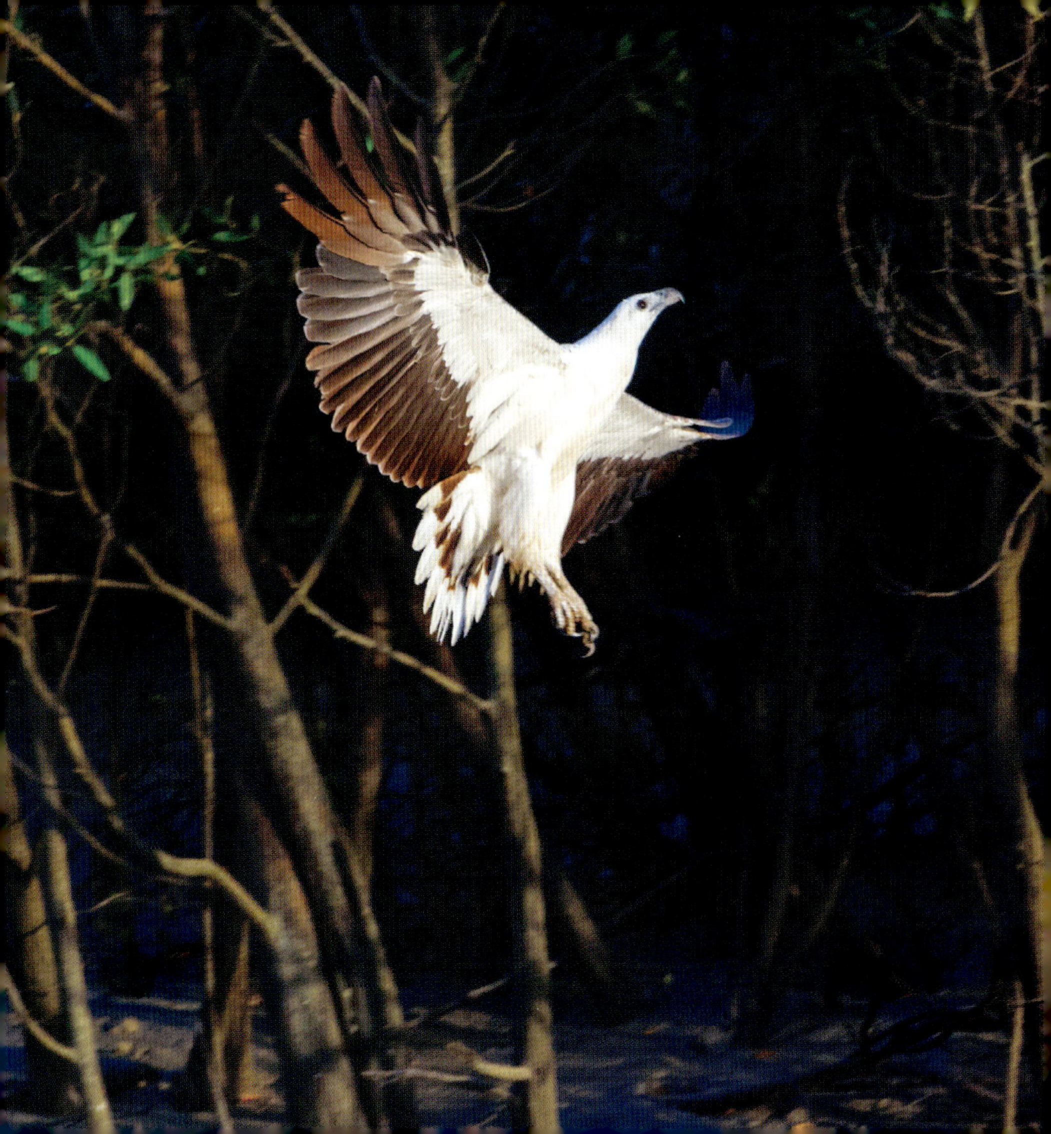

Forgiveness

Forgive yourself and
  release any feelings of guilt

Look truthfully at your
  feelings of a past hurt you
    haven't been able to forgive

Confess your part in a conflict
  and make amends

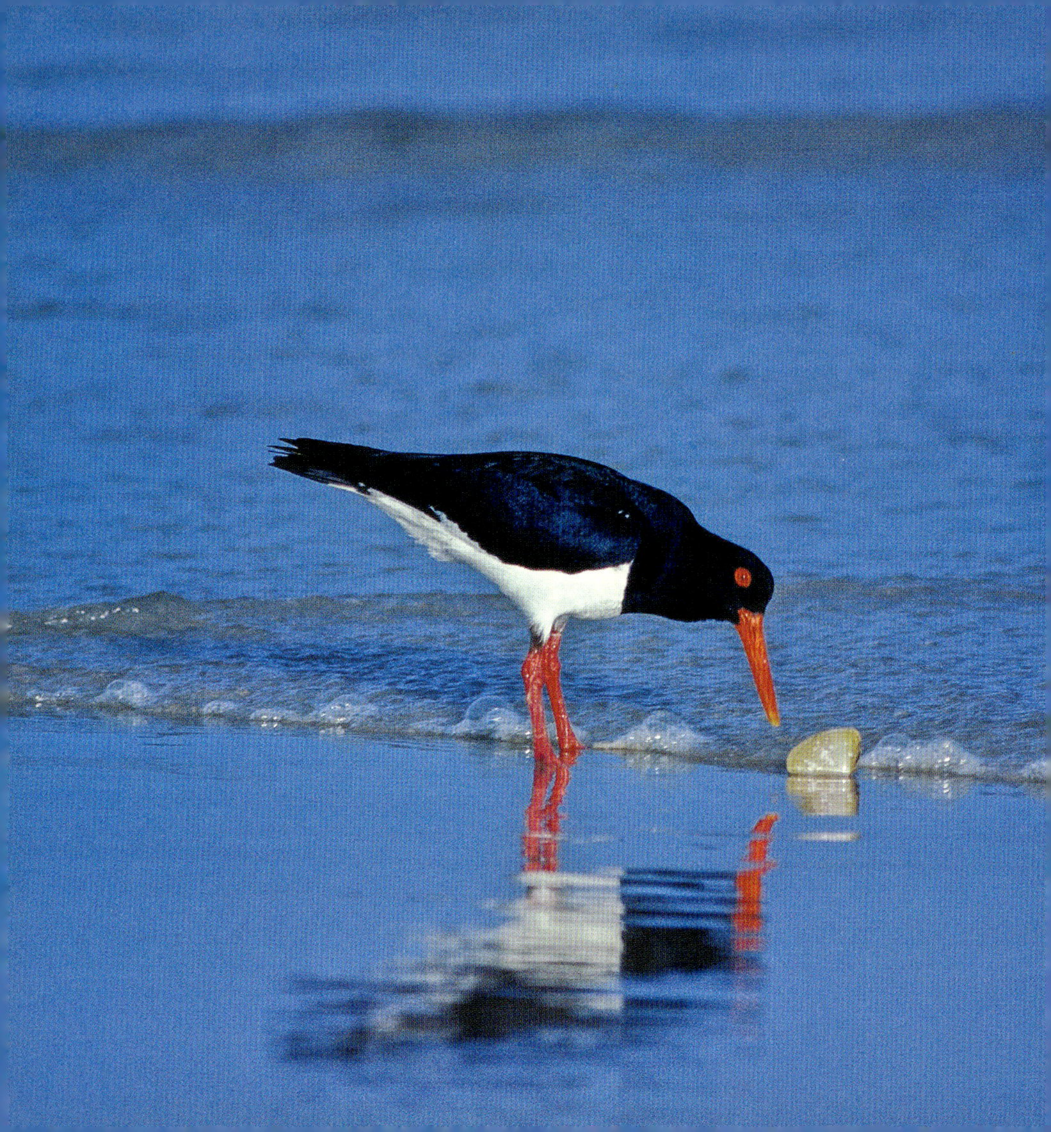

Consideration

*Consideration for others
is the basis of a good life, a good society.*

CONFUCIUS

Consideration in every action, every word, and every thought will bring a good attitude to your life. A good attitude is a compassionate one where the wellbeing of others and the planet is equal to your own.

A mindful moment for

Consideration

*Have awareness of the nature
of your words and actions*

*Be present and thus considerate
of others in crowded places*

*Consider the natural environment
and clean up any litter*

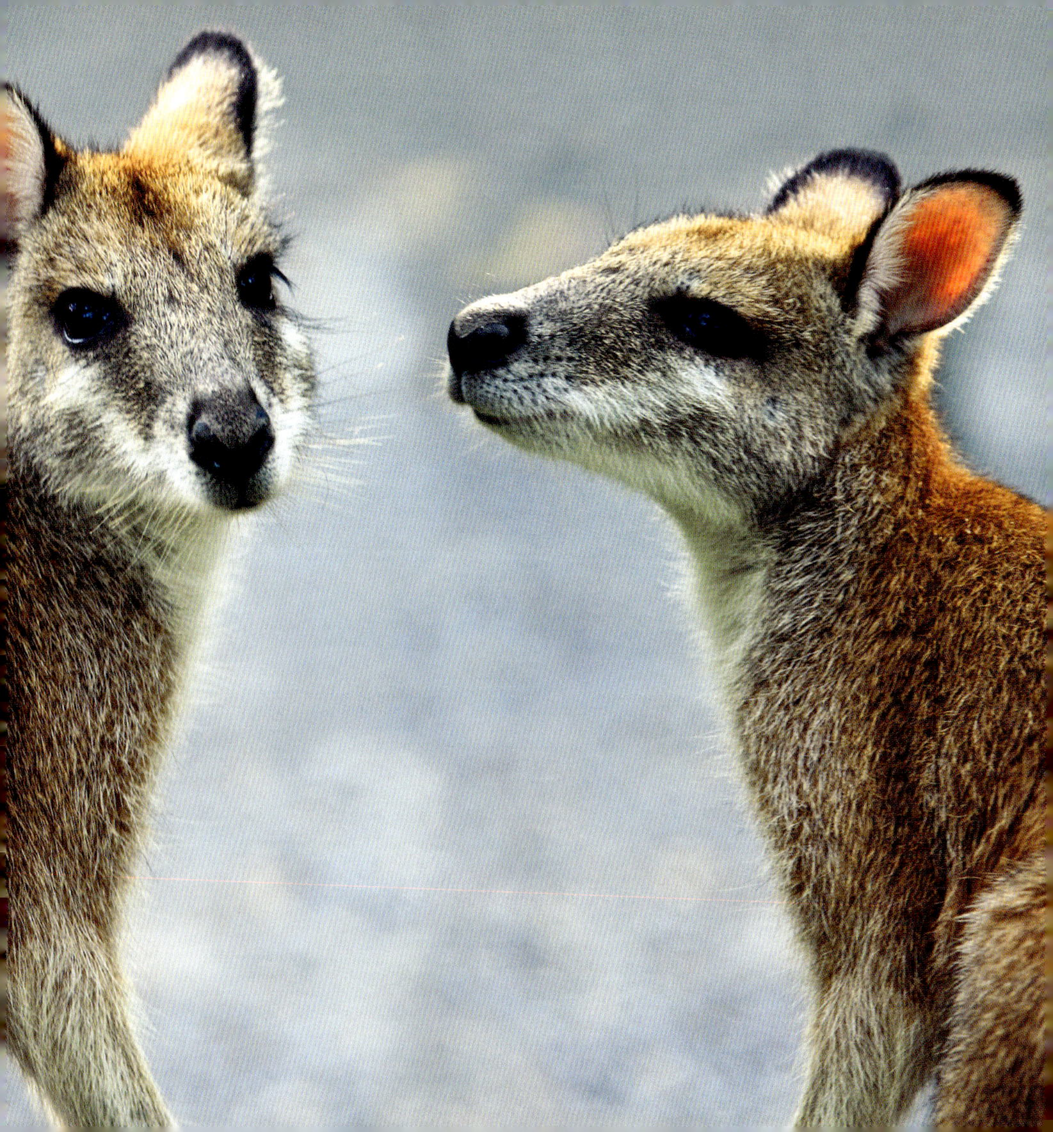

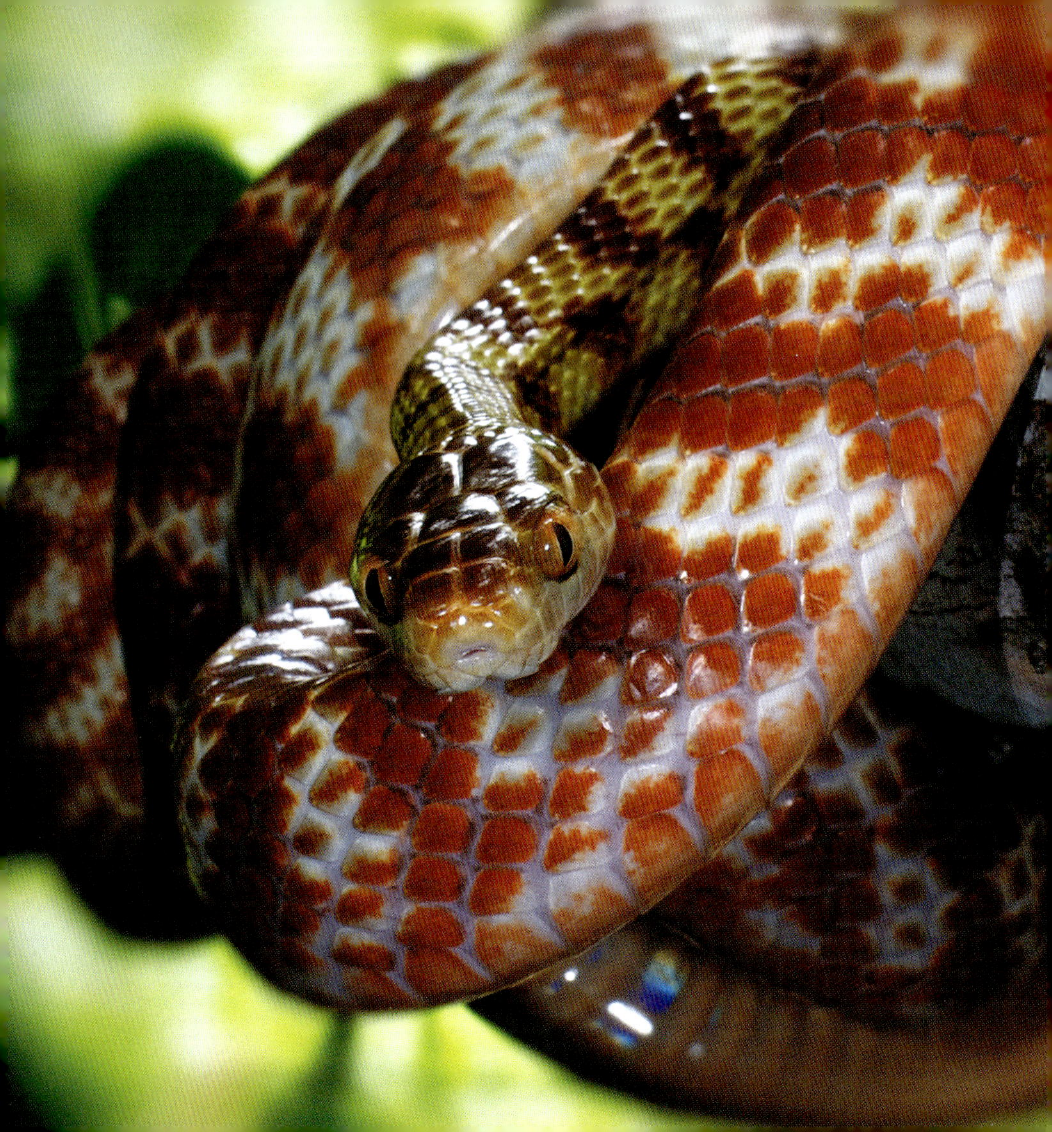

Embracing

Our task must be to free ourselves ... by widening our circle of compassion to embrace all living creatures and the whole of nature and its beauty.

ALBERT EINSTEIN

Embrace all that happens to you with an attitude of detachment. Life happens — it is a series of events, a part of human existence. Embrace each event, person and experience as if they were personally chosen for you to optimise the experience of your life. Embrace life in every expression!

Take a moment for

Embracing

Consider a 'bad' event from your past as a learning *opportunity*

Be *grateful* for the existence of all creatures on our planet

Embrace your inner and outer *beauty*

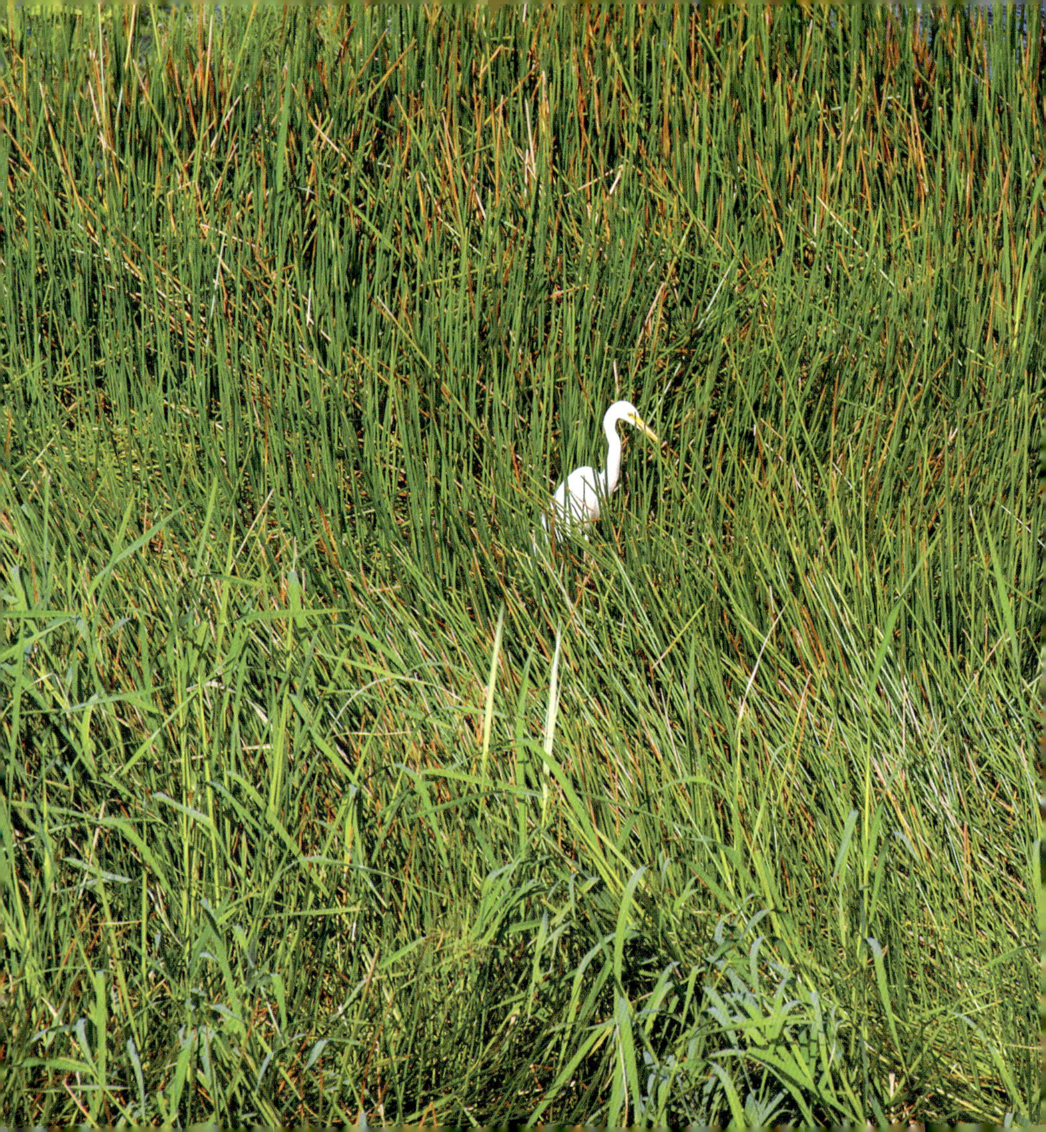

Peace

*If we have no peace,
it is because we have forgotten that we
belong to each other.*

MOTHER TERESA

Peace exists in the present moment. The mind stops processing, emotions are in abeyance and the heart is wide open to what is.

Take a moment for

Peace

*Take a moment to bring peace
to a stressful situation or person*

*Know that every deep breath will
slow you down and return you to
a centred and balanced place*

*Sitting in nature makes
feeling peaceful easier*

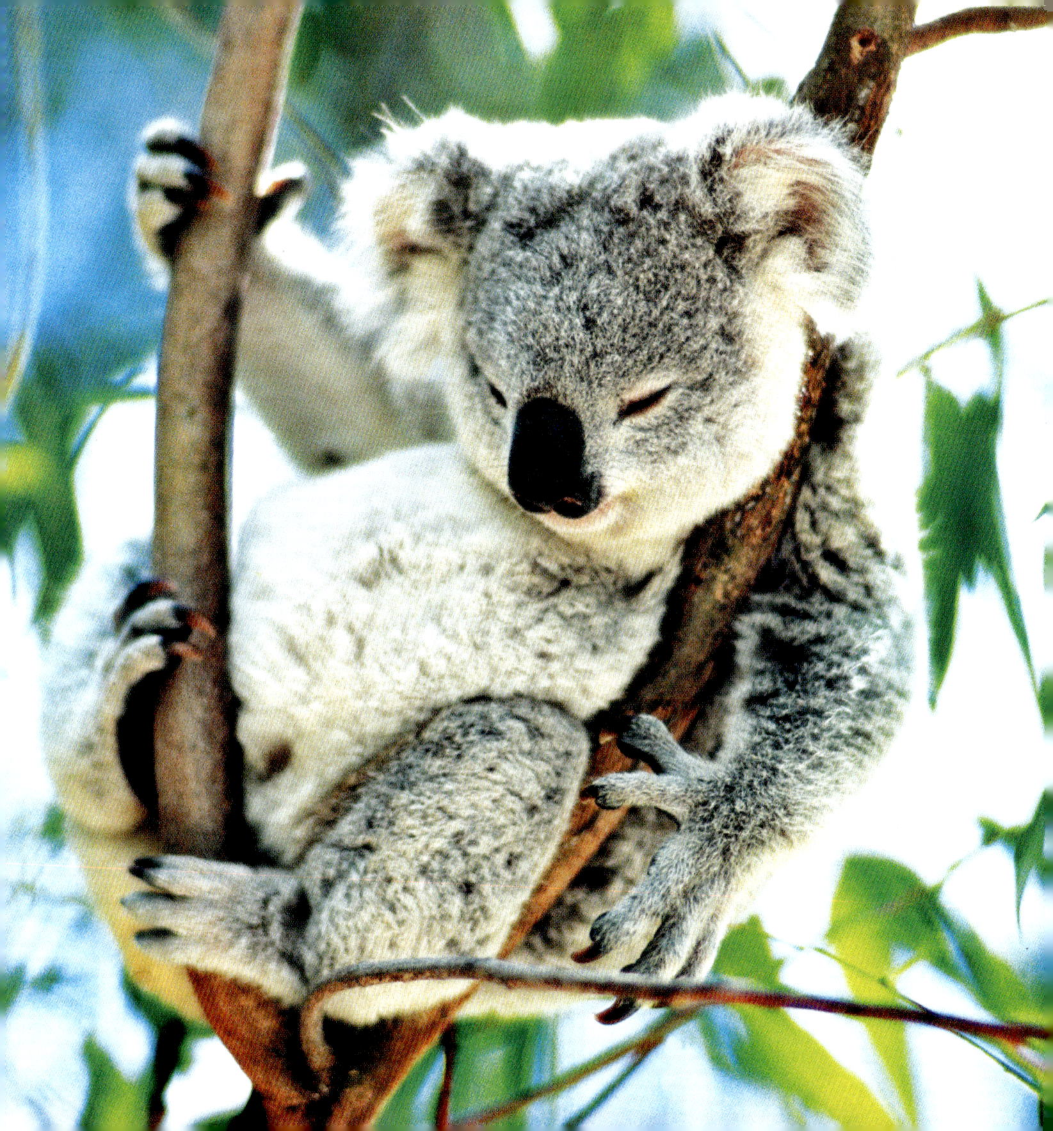

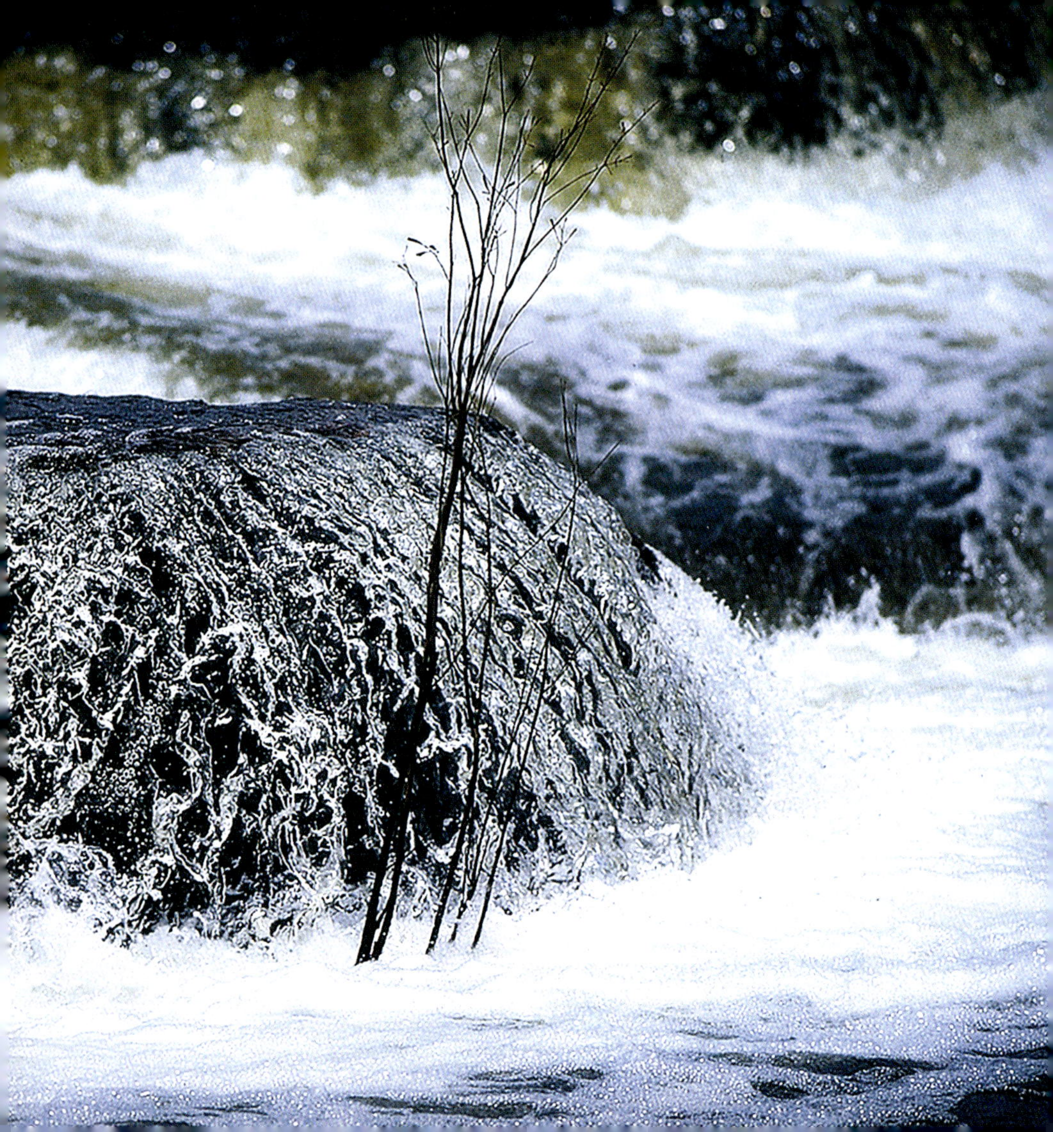

Trust

*I trust that everything happens for a reason,
even if we are not wise enough to see it.*

OPRAH WINFREY

Trust enables us to discover our own path to 'consciousness'. Trust in the events that are in front of you. Believe life gets better and it will, for what you focus on is most usually what you get. When your focus is on attaining a balanced, compassionate life, your heart will open and compassion will flow.

Take a moment for
Trust

A wild animal who turns his back on you trusts you.
Try it. He still has an ear of awareness on you.

Suspend negative thought and dive into life

If trust fails, open your heart and trust again

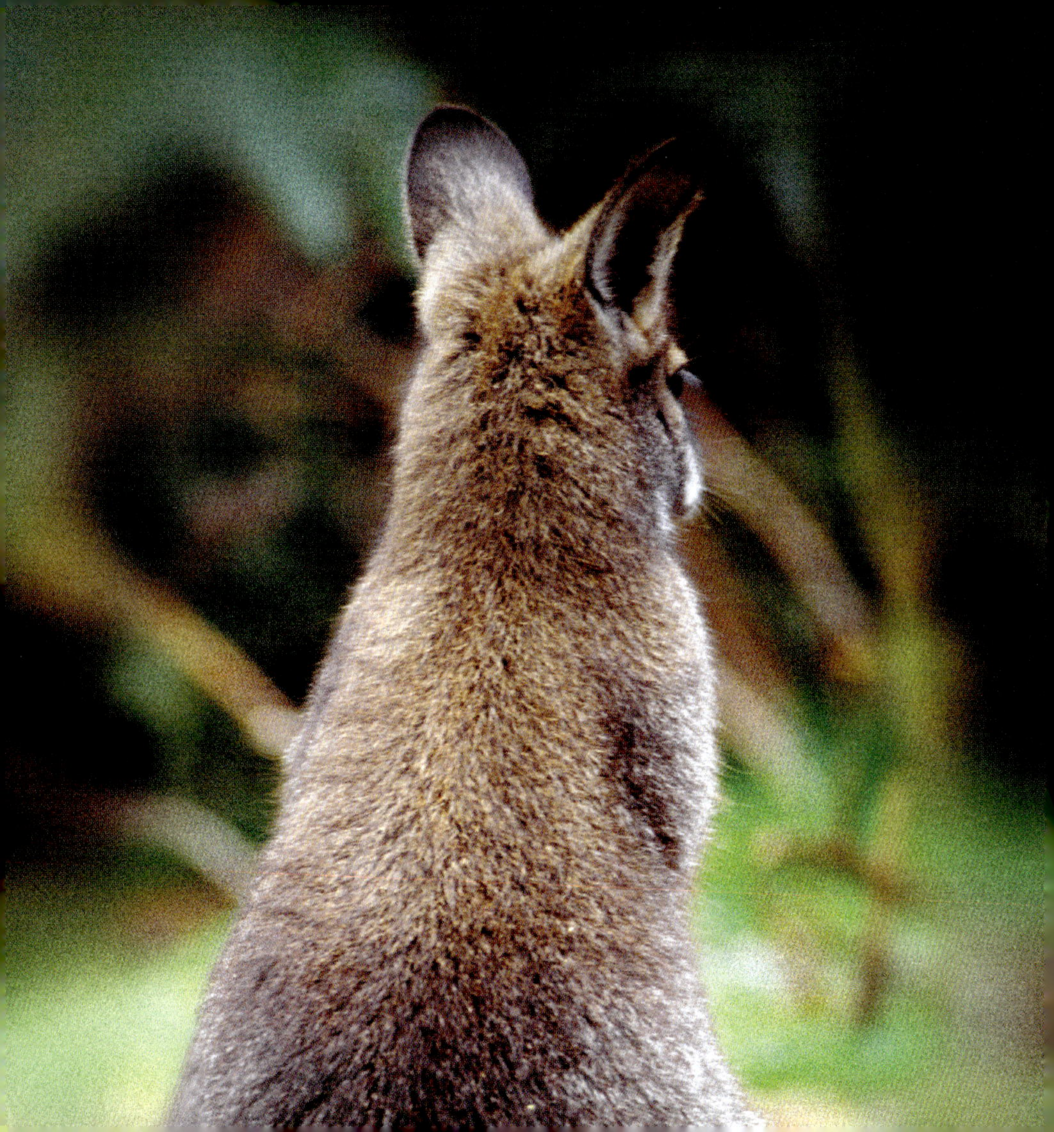

Open-hearted

*When the heart speaks,
the mind finds it indecent to object.*

MILAN KUNDERA

Get in touch with your senses (not emotions) and intuit your way through life. Let your heart rule your head.

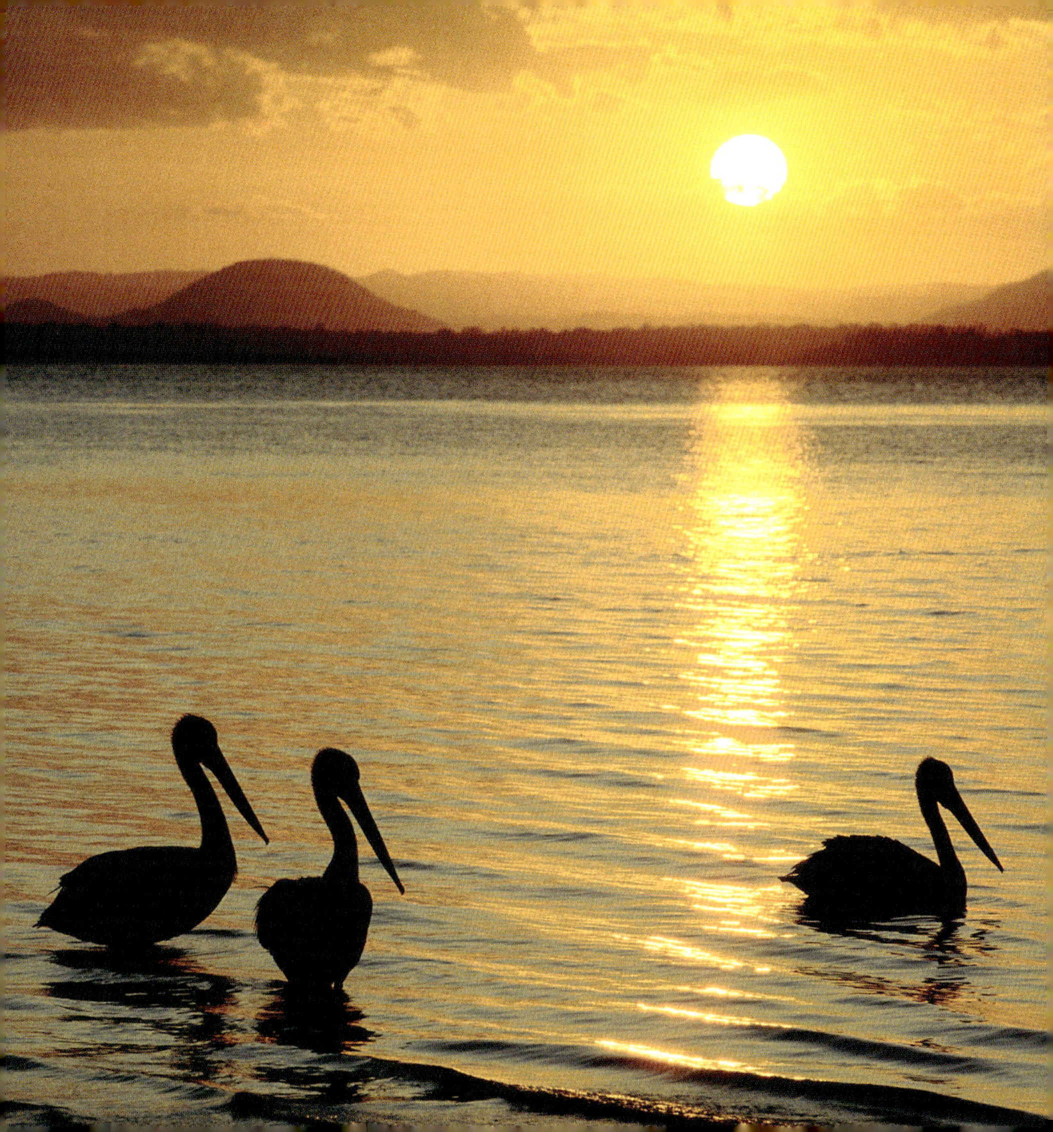

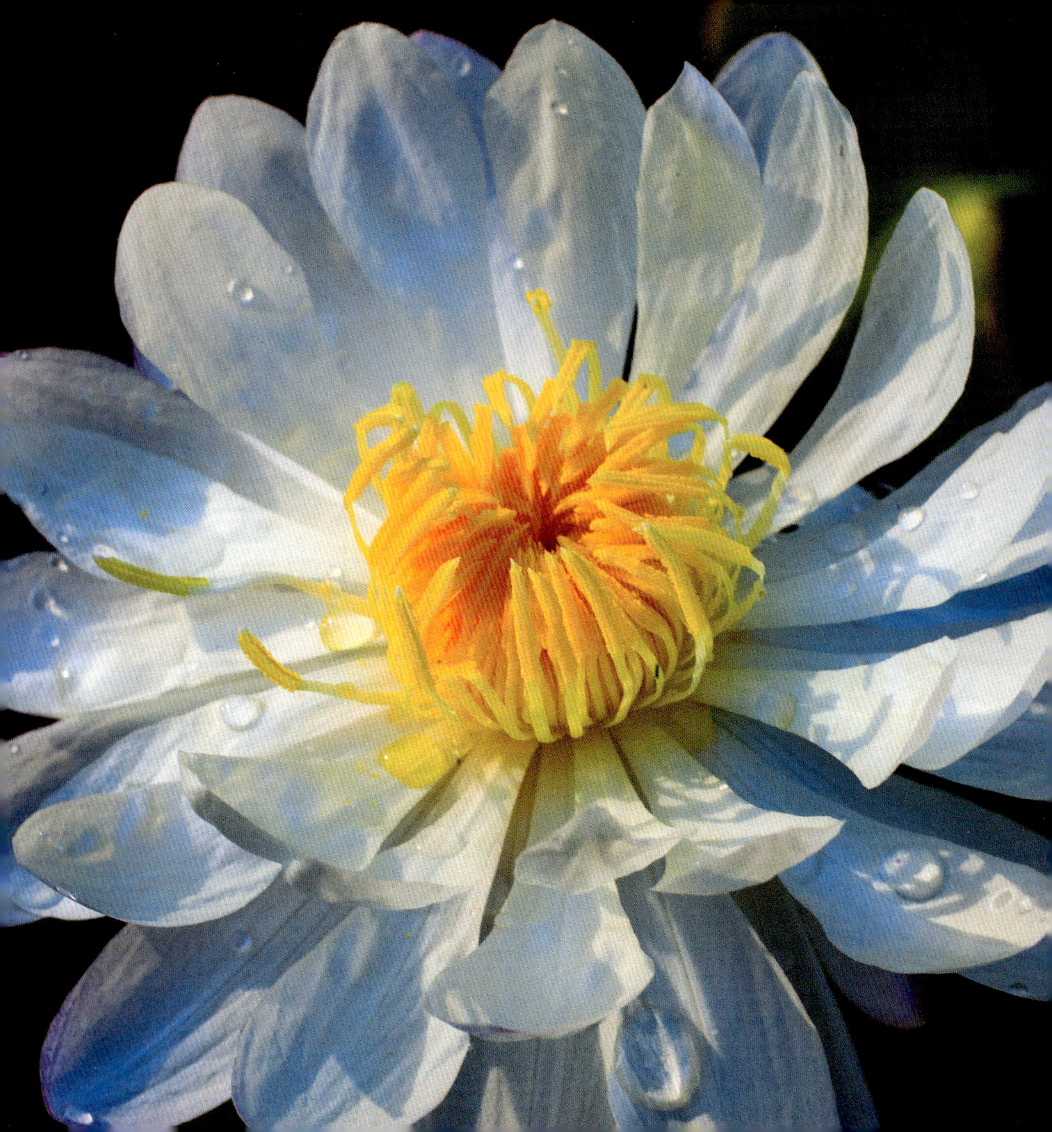

Take a moment for

Open-heartedness

Accept and **embrace** *what IS to feel your heart open*

Feel the **beauty** *of the natural
world with your heart*

Hold **compassion** *in your heart
for those who are suffering*

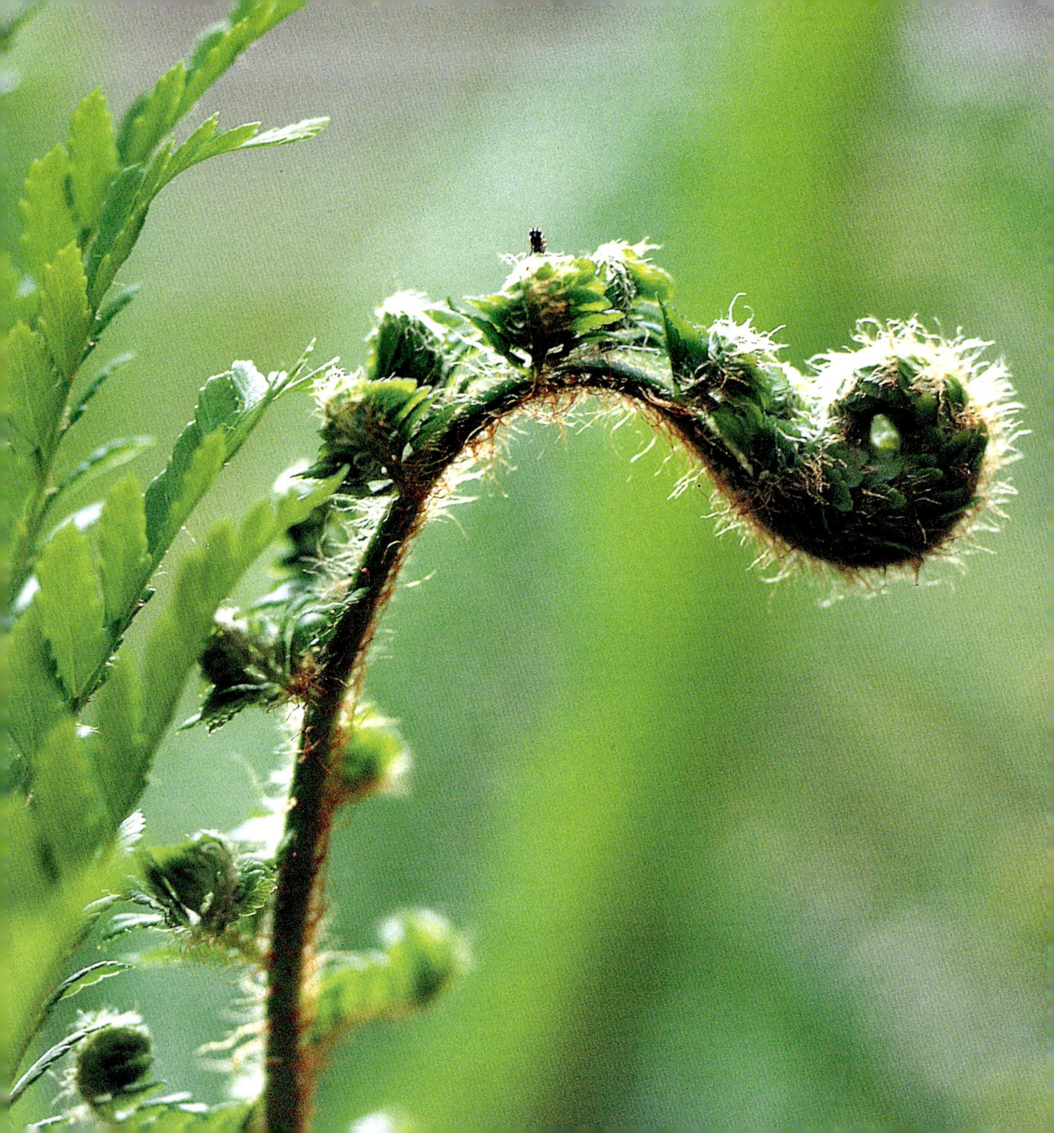

Awakened

I may not have gone where I intended to go,
but I think I have ended up where I needed to be.

DOUGLAS ADAMS

When we reside in an awakened state, we are full of love and compassion. We feel peace in the present moment, we trust open-heartedly with a balanced sense of self, we are at ease with our existence and we feel a strong sense of connection with the world and its inhabitants.

A mindful moment for
Wakefulness

Practise mental **quietness**
while moving with awareness

Find the **space** *just before*
your next thought arrives

Get up early and watch the
sun rising *on a new day*

INSPIRED BY NATURE

First published 2013.

Published by Pascal Press
PO Box 250, Glebe, NSW 2037 Australia

© copyright 2013 Pascal Press
Photography and text © Nature-Connect Pty Ltd

ISBN 9781922225047

All rights reserved. No part of this publication may be reproduced, stored in a retrieval system, transmitted in any form or by any means, electronic, mechanical, photocopying, recording or otherwise without the prior permission in writing of the publisher.

Photography: Steve Parish
Authors: Steve Parish & Kate Prentice
Publisher: Lynn Dickinson
Designer: Leanne Nobilio
Editors: Marie Theodore, Vanessa Barker

Printed in China.

www.steveparish.com.au